AMERICA'S CHANGE

A POETIC VIEW

ARNITA L. FIELDS

2009 Copyright © by Arnita L. Fields
All rights reserved, including the right to reproduce this book or potions thereof in any form by any means, electronic, mechanical, photocopy, recording, or otherwise; without prior written consent of the publisher. For information address Holy Poetry Publications, PO Box 754301 Memphis, TN 38175

First Printing

All scripture and references are taken from the New King James Version of the bible. Copyright © 1985 Thomas Nelson Publishers, Inc. Used by permission. All rights reserved.

ISBN # 978-0-578-03210-8
Published by Holy Poetry Publications
Memphis, Tennessee
www.holypoetrypublications.net

Printed in the United States of America

AMERICA'S CHANGE

A POETIC VIEW

Contents

- 12 When Interruptions Come
- 13 America's Change
- 14 Obama's New Day
- 16 The Days of Yesterday
- 17 A Road Traveled
- 18 The Struggle is over
- 20 Transformation
- 21 Embrace the Change
- 22 New Sight
- 24 Not about Me
- 25 A Life on Loan
- 26 Pursuit of Liberty
- 28 Grace
- 29 Back in God's Arms Again
- 30 Sun Arising
- 32 A Poetic View (Essay)
- 36 Breathe on Me
- 37 Sweet Holy Spirit (Spiritual Song)

INTRODUCTION

2 Chronicles 7:14-15 "If my people who are called by my name will humble themselves, and pray and seek my face, and turn from their wicked ways, then I will hear from heaven, and will forgive their sin and heal their land. Now my eyes will be open and my ears attentive to prayer made in this place."

Restoration Prayer

Father God, we humble our hearts and align our minds and spirit with you, the only true and living God. We ask that you forgive us for the times we have missed you and allowed our fleshly desires to cloud our thoughts and lives with things which took our focus from true kingdom business. God we repent for all of the negative and unholy things we as a people have allowed to enter into our country and communities. Many of the things we have allowed could have been prevented if we as a people had taken out time to petition your throne of grace.

Heavenly Father, we repent for the murder of every unborn child who will never have an opportunity to experience life. We repent for allowing prayer to be taken out of our public schools and for allowing the enemy free access to our children's lives. Forgive us God for abusing the elderly and for mistreating the poor and disenfranchised. We repent for not truly loving our neighbors as ourselves. Forgive us dear God for all of our selfishness and for only being concerned about our individual needs. So many people are hurting and dying right before our eyes because we have not been true lights upon a hill, but more like pen lights in a dense fog. Father, please forgive us for our spiritual blindness. Open our eyes so we may see our country and the world through your eyes.

Father God, forgive us for sleeping on the job and for wasting precious time. We repent for not standing in the gap and interceding for our government leaders and those who have rule over us. Forgive us for our constant complaining and bickering and for not participating in our country's growth process. Your word tells us to work while it is yet day, for when the night comes no man can work. Breathe on us God, so the flame in our hearts will burn with a new intensity and fire as we set our hands to help complete the work that you have already started in this country. May our eyes be focused as we renew our commitment to serve you God in not only words but in faith and godly works. Father God, we humbly accept this new challenge as our country unites to walk into this new season of change. Thank you for forgiving us for our sins and iniquities and also for directing us back to your heart and into your divine will and purpose for America.

We thank you for hearing our prayer and for not casting us away from your presence. We do honor and reverence your most holy name, for you are a God of a second chance. May your kingdom come and your divine will be done on earth as it is in heaven. In Jesus name we do decree and declare that America does belong to the most High God, Amen.

Special Thanks

To my incredible and awesome Heavenly Father, you are indeed my source and my strength.

To my husband, Anthony thanks for just being you.

To my fellow Americans who have desired to embrace God's change, and who are willing to turn their hearts completely back to Him.

To Ms. Evelyn Willis, the Assistant Principal and to the 5th grade students in the 2008 Author's Workshop at Oakhaven Elementary (Memphis, TN). Thanks for inspiring me with your dedication and passion for writing.

To my former co-workers (especially on the 3rd floor), thanks for supporting my writing projects. God is able to do more than you can even hope for or imagine.

SCENE ONE

When Interruptions Come

America's Change 2008

Obama's New Day

When Interruptions Come

There are moments that come when I don't even have a clue,
and I don't even realize that some things do come from you.

Many of the things that come my way to sway my faith,
seem to have the enemy's fingerprints all over the place.

But I know that my times, they are in your hands,
with each new day as I walk out your plans.

When interruptions come to disrupt my life,
help me to understand and not always put up a fight.

Your plans are to prosper me and not to bring me harm,
for it's in the center of your will, that I will be safe in your loving arms.

America's Change 2008

Just as a river passes and flows into the sea,
a new day is dawning full of faith for both you and me.

A time of new discoveries, a time of new ideas,
it is a time of great celebration after many, many dark years.

Take the limits off your heart and allow your mind to unwind.

There's a season of change happening today in America, and
I know that it is right on time.

Obama's New Day

Destined for greatness despite the many obstacles he has faced.

God created and formed him as a part of the human race.

He's made in his image, shaped by God's very own hands.

It's such an honor to be called upon as God's very own man. God knew what he had to go through to get to this very place.

Everyday was a part of a larger than life puzzle base with each piece going into its own special place.

His steps have been ordered, although many times he did not understand.

The ups and downs and in betweens were all part of God's master plan. His purpose is not completely fulfilled; in fact it's only just begun.

There's still change coming for him today, and it's available to each and everyone.

SCENE TWO

The Days of Yesterday

A Road Traveled

The Struggle is over

The Days of Yesterday

The days of yesterday seems so far away, when I stepped out of the world's mold looking for a change.

The days of yesterday seems so far away, when I surrendered my life to serve people God's way.

The days of yesterday seems so far away, when I opened my eyes to see the brightness of the day.

Today, as I look back it's no longer a dream; my past and my future are now fused together, working in perfect harmony.

A Road Traveled

Many have gone before me, too many to even name.

There are many who have gone before me, who helped to labor for a change.

Many have gone before me who were bruised, beat and stabbed.

Yes, there are many who have gone before me, on whose shoulders I now stand.

The Struggle is over

The door has swung open to a brand new day.

Lights, camera's, action, chase all of the clouds away.

Newsflash, Newsflash, its extra extra, read all about it.

History is now being made, different from our past.

The struggle is over, break forth from your chains.

This storyline is different from all of the other days.

Shout hallelujah, no more boundaries for me.

A new day is coming, and it is completely drama free.

SCENE THREE

Transformation

Embrace the Change

New Sight

Transformation

We are transformed by the renewing of our minds.

Our surrender is important, especially during this time.

Shake off the offences and all of the pain too.

The Lord God will guide us, all of the way through.

Our testimony is true and our time has now come.

There's more to this victory than done under this sun.

Liberated and set free, from the mindsets of our past history.

We are indeed transformed by the renewing of our minds.

Embrace the Change

Change is good, and it can come at any given time.
Many times unexpected when we think were doing just fine.

God knows our hearts and the test of our wills,
He has it all under control, relax now and be still.

The time has now come for America's brand new day.

After this special time people, we will never be the same.

Many will ask how could this happen?
I don't want this change.

But contrary to popular opinions,
God does not feel the same way.

He sets men in order and puts one up and takes one down,
change is not dictated by our feelings or common ground.

Embrace the change; it will be good for your soul.
God the Father is not the author of confusion, so release now
your hold.

New Sight

I can see clearly now because the rain has gone.

The fog has lifted and I'm on my way home.

I roll down my windows and take in the entire breeze, the wind is so fresh now, that it fills me up with peace.

It does not matter, the many miles that are facing me.

I have come this far by faith, and will certainly reach my destiny.

SCENE FOUR

Not About Me

A Life on Loan

Pursuit of Liberty

Not about Me

It is not about me. It is not about me, but Jesus.

It is not about me. It is not about me, but Jesus.

It is not about my will, my wants or my needs.

It is all about others who are waiting to be free.

People are looking for a way of escape, although many times their problems are the ones that they made.

I offer up my heart, my hands and my feet too, to be an extension of God and to show forth His mercy, in all that I say and do.

It is not about me. It is not about me, but Jesus.

A Life on Loan

A life on loan, I am not my own.

I was bought with a price, God's own sacrifice.

Shed His blood for more than one, not only for me, but it was because of His love.

God is the potter, I am the clay, shaped and molded in His own special way.

My life, my dreams don't mean a thing, if all I care about is how to please me.

Today, I surrender my life and my thoughts, seeking to please God in the way that I walk and talk.

I'm commanded to love God and others as I would myself.

My life is now a life on loan to bless others, just as Jesus came and lived himself.

How will you live your life today for God?

Pursuit of Liberty

Searching for something you are not even sure exists.

Is it just in your imagination or something you have already missed?

Searching deeper and deeper, now into a well you go.

Are you stepping outside your boundaries trying to reach your goal?

Down in your spirit, you know you are destined for change.

Is the pursuit of liberty worth the cost or should you just remain the same?

SCENE FIVE

Grace

Back in God's Arms Again

Sun Arising

Grace

It is another chance, another opportunity, another day to stand.

It is an honor and a privilege to live in this land.

We could have been born in some far away place, instead of in a country so full of God's grace.

America, o how we do not deserve to be blessed this much, by a faithful and loving Father who warms us with His touch.

Father, forgive us for taking advantage of your grace, today we repent and now turn to seek your holy face.

Back in God's Arms Again

I've been gone away too long, on the road because I left home.

Met up with people who lived a life of sin, who did not even care about what was going on.

I was lost and began to spiral further into a hole; on the way to hell was my soul.

I then met up with friends from my past who took me in; this was my way of escape from the darkness within.

They prayed for and covered me, kept me warm from the elements of the streets.

Now I'm on my way back to the place I came from, a place that's full of grace so sweet.

Father forgive me for my many sins, I repent of them now from the beginning to the end.

I want to stay free from the ills of this society. I want to be back in your loving arms again.

Sun Arising

Bright lights coming forth, moving across the sky,
rays of sunshine everywhere; opening up blinded eyes.

It's a new day dawning, the brightness now covers me,
God's righteousness and His glory have come to set us free.

No one can escape the brightness of the sun.

Glory, Honor, Dominion and Power belongs to the Most Holy one.

The sun is arising, on the wings of the morn.

A special day has come to stay,
a new era has now begun.

SCENE SIX

A Poetic View
Essay

A Poetic View

When I look at America the country that I have been created and ordained to live and work in, I see many things. I see a country that is so full and rich with possibilities, that it overflows to the outside of our borders and then out into the ocean. I see a country that was started on the principle that without God at the center of everything, we as a country would not make it, period. I see a country so full and deep with wisdom that no one could mistakenly say that God was not a part of our very foundation. America, God has poured out His spirit in you for over two hundred years, He cares about where we are now, and where we are going as a people. God has continued to this very day to call out our name, day after day after day; America are we willing to answer His call?

America when I look at you, I see a country that has a heart to reach out to help others when they are hurting and left without hope. I see a country that not only raises money and offers monetary support to other countries, but also supports many less than fortunate countries with brotherly protection.

Looking deep into the heart of America, I see an assortment of people who have come from many nations seeking a place of refuge, and a place of safety from the raging storms of life. I see a country where people are drawn like a magnet to its shores, year after year.

So what is it about this country that we call America? What's so different about America in comparison to any other country in the whole wide world? Well, you may say that it is because people can come and experience freedom like they have never known before. Many will speak about the endless opportunities that people can have to provide for their families, so they can enjoy the many pleasures of life. But what does God say about America?

America, God has never let you out of His sight although you may have felt forsaken at times. God has divine plans for you. His plans are to prosper you and not to harm you but to give you a future and a hope. America, if you truly repent and turn back from the ways of the world and direct your whole heart back to the Almighty Sovereign God, then you will see the very best of our country.

America the beautiful, a county so full of God's love and His grace, know that God loves you and He desires to see you become all that His hands has created and designed you to become. God has invested so much in our country since its birth over two hundred years ago. It is time to reclaim our heritage and return to our roots. America, are you ready for your change?

2 Chronicles 7:14-15 "If my people who are called by my name will humble themselves, and pray and seek my face, and turn from their wicked ways, then I will hear from heaven, and will forgive their sin and heal their land. Now my eyes will be open and my ears attentive to prayer made in this place."

SCENE SEVEN

Breathe on Me

Sweet Holy Spirit

Breathe on Me

Gentle wisps of air cross over my eyes,

my lips began to smile as I sing a tune inside my head.

The zest of life is mine o mine.

It's no longer a secret how God makes me come alive.

I am truly free, as He breathes upon me,

no longer on the life support of society.

Sweet Holy Spirit
(Spiritual Song)

Sweet Holy Spirit, o how you are welcome, o how you are welcome in this place.

Sweet Holy Spirit come fall upon us, fall upon us in this place.

Sweet Holy Spirit, lead us closer, come lead us closer in this place.

Speak forth what you hear from the throne room, speak forth what God wants us to know.

Reveal the plans of God our Father, reveal the way back into His loving arms.

Sweet Holy Spirit, o how you are welcome, o how you are welcome in this place.

Sweet Holy Spirit, come shower us with our Father's grace.

FINALE

Spiritual Food

Spiritual Food for the Soul

Isaiah 1:18   Come now, and let us reason together, says the Lord. Though your sins are like scarlet, they shall be white as snow.

Psalm 51:1-2   Have mercy upon me, O God, according to your loving kindness, according to the multitude of your tender mercies.   Blot out my transgressions.   Wash me thoroughly from my iniquity, and cleanse me from my sin.

Psalm 51:10-11   Create in me a clean heart, o God, and renew a steadfast spirit within me.   Do not cast me away from your presence, and do not take your Holy Spirit from me.

Psalm 63:1   O God, you are my God; early will I seek you.

Lamentations 5:21   Turn us back to You, O Lord, and we will be restored.

Psalm 116:12-13   What shall I render to the Lord for all His benefits towards me? I will take up the cup of salvation and call upon the name of the Lord.

Psalm 42:1-2   As the deer pants for the water brooks, so pants my soul for You, O God. My soul thirsts for God, for the living God.

Another Helping

John 3:16   For God so loved the world that He gave His only begotten Son, that whoever believes in Him should not perish but have everlasting life.

John 3:17   For God did not send His Son into the world to condemn the world, but that the world through Him might be saved.

2 Peter 3:9   The Lord is not slack concerning His promise, as some count slackness, but He is longsuffering towards us, not willing that any should perish but that all should come to repentance.

Ephesians 1:7   In Him we have redemption through His blood, the forgiveness of sins, according to the riches of His grace.

1 Corinthians 10:13   No temptation has overtaken you except such as is common to man; but God is faithful, who will not allow you to be tempted beyond what you are able, but with the temptation will also make the way of escape, that you may be able to bear it.

1 John 5:4-5   For whatever is born of God overcomes the world. And this is the victory that has overcome the world our faith. Who is he who overcomes the world, but he who believes that Jesus is the Son of God?

Prayer of Salvation

If after reading this book, you have a desire to know Jesus as your personal Lord and Savior, please pray the following prayer:

*I repent of all of my sins and right now I do confess that Jesus is the Son of God and that He died for the remission of my sins. I believe that Jesus died and was buried and rose again, and is now seated at the right hand of God in Heaven. I receive Him now as Lord of my life and I now commit to serve him for the rest of my days.
It's in Jesus name I do pray, Amen*

If you have just prayed this prayer and want more information about beginning your new life as a Christian, please call or write us, we will be happy to send you a free booklet.

Holy Poetry Publications
PO BOX 754301
Memphis, TN 38175
Email: arnitafields@yahoo.com
Web: www.holypoetrypublications.net
901.786.3519

Other books by author Arnita L. Fields

Rescued, Restored, Renewed and Revived
A Collection of Christian Poems

And the Beat Goes On
Includes Poems from a Restored Marriage

This Far By Faith
Anthology
(Contributing Author)

THE WORD
A Poetry Connection

Revive Your Marriage Covenant
A Guide for Separated Couples
Co-Authored with husband Anthony J. Fields
(Coming 2010)

Holy Poetry
Flowing thru my mind
(Coming 2010)

Order Form

To order extra copies of ***America's Change a Poetic View***
please mail your orders to:

Holy Poetry Publications
P. O. Box 754301
Memphis, TN 38175
901.786.3519

I would like to order _____ copies of America's Change a Poetic View @ **$ 9.00** each
Please include **$ 2.50** per book for shipping and handling

Order Total $_____

Please make all money orders payable to
Holy Poetry Publications. *Please do not send cash.*

Shipping Address

Name _____
Address _____
City, State, Zip _____
Phone Number ( ) _____

About the Author

Poet, writer and author, Arnita L. Fields is also a minister of the gospel who teaches the word of God with clarity and simplicity. She has a burning passion and desire to see that all marriages in the body of Christ operate and function in the divine order of God. Arnita is a full time student pursuing a degree in Psychology, with a future goal of counseling troubled marriages. She has been married to her husband Anthony for twelve years.

Contact Information

www.arnitalfields.net
www.holypoetrypublications.net
arnitafields@yahoo.com
info@holypoetrypublications.net
901.786.3519

To schedule Arnita L. Fields for your next ministry event please use the contact information listed above. To schedule Arnita for your next literary event, you may contact Sherita Redic at: info@sredicpublicity.net

www.ingramcontent.com/pod-product-compliance
Lightning Source LLC
Chambersburg PA
CBHW031437040426
42444CB00006B/859